Praise the Lord, My Soul

For Mariah

Text copyright © 2002 by Christopher L. Webber
Illustrations copyright © 2002 by Preston McDaniels

Morehouse Publishing
P.O. Box 1321
Harrisburg, PA 17105

Morehouse Publishing is a CONTINUUM IMPRINT

Cover design by Corey Kent
Page design by Brenda Klinger

A catalog record of this book is available from the Library of Congress.

ISBN 0-8192-1889-8

Printed in Malaysia
03 04 05 06   6 5 4 3 2

Praise the Lord, My Soul

Psalm 104 for Children

Retold by
Christopher L. Webber

Illustrated by
Preston McDaniels

MOREHOUSE PUBLISHING
Harrisburg, Pennsylvania

Praise the Lord, O my soul,
Your name is very great.
You wrap yourself up in sunlight like a robe.

You spread out the sky like a tent above us.
The clouds become your chariot;
the winds become your messengers.

You set the earth in place
and covered it with the deep sea,
which rises and falls at your command.

You made the shoreline that divides the land from the water
to keep the waves from covering the earth.

You make the rain fall on the hills
and the streams run down to the valleys.
You make the springs bubble up
so wild animals can drink when they are thirsty.

*B*irds build their nests in the trees
and sing their songs on the branches.

You make the grass grow to feed the horses and cows,
and plants for us to eat.
You provide good things for us to drink
and bread to make us strong.

Wild goats find homes in the high mountains,
and the little rabbits hide between the rocks.

You gave us the moon to show us the seasons.
The sun sets to bring the darkness
so animals in the forest
can hunt for their food.

*T*he lions roar
as they hunt for the food God gives them.
When morning comes, they go back to their dens
while men and women get up and go to work.

Lord God, how many things you have made,
and how well you have planned it all!
The earth is filled with all you have made.

You filled the great, wide sea with living things
both large and small.
The ships sail on the sea and Leviathan plays in it,
the monster you made for the fun of it.

All living things look to you for their food.
You open your hands
and fill us with good things.

May God be happy to look at all creation,
may I please God in everything I think and do.

I will sing songs of praise to God the creator;
as long as I live I will sing God's praise.
Let us always give God praise.

Christopher L. Webber is the author of over a dozen books, and his hymns appear in several major hymnals. He has ministered to inner city, suburban, and overseas parishes, and currently serves two small congregations in rural northwestern Connecticut. He has been married for over 40 years to Margaret Elisabeth Webber; they have four grown children and three grandchildren.

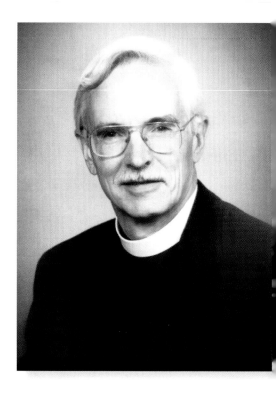

Preston McDaniels' interest in art began as a young child when he entertained himself by drawing. He also fell in love with music as a child, and still plays his trusty piano each morning. He combined his love of music and his talent for illustration in four critically acclaimed books of hymns for children, *God of the Sparrow*, *All Things Bright and Beautiful*, *Earth & All Stars*, and *Now the Day Is Over*, all available from Morehouse Publishing. He lives in Nebraska with his wife Cindy and two daughters, Abby and Lizzie.

Photo by Hal Maggiore